MASTER THEORY

Intermediate Theory Workbook

by Charles S. Peters and Paul Yoder

The Second Workbook in the MASTER THEORY SERIES

CONTENTS

ISBN 0-8497-0155-4

Lesson 31

THE KEY SIGNATURE

Sharps and flats immediately following the clef sign are called the key signature. These accidentals effect every note on the line or space which they represent throughout the entire piece of music unless they are cancelled by a natural sign (♮) or a change to another key.

In the following example, every note called F is now raised one half-step to F# because a sharp is placed on the F line in the key signature.

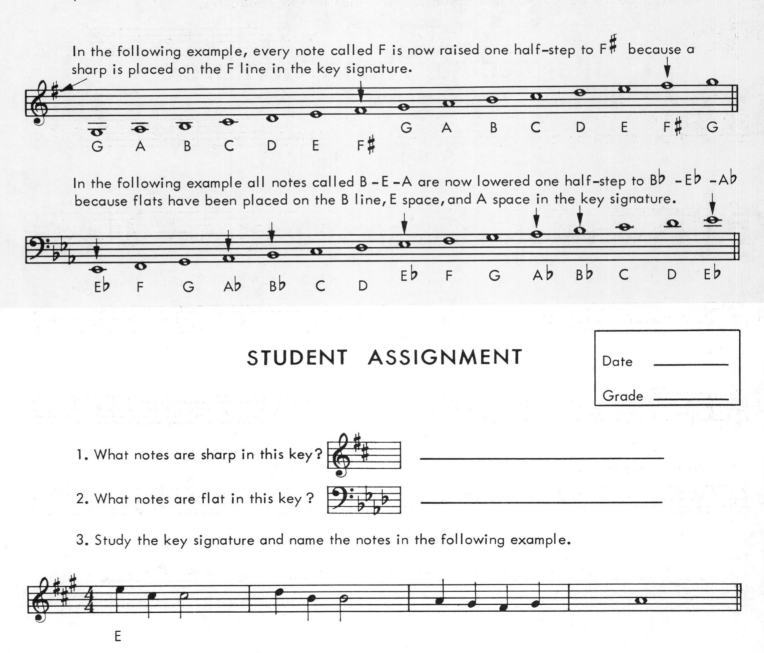

In the following example all notes called B – E – A are now lowered one half-step to B♭ – E♭ – A♭ because flats have been placed on the B line, E space, and A space in the key signature.

STUDENT ASSIGNMENT

Date _____

Grade _____

1. What notes are sharp in this key? _____

2. What notes are flat in this key? _____

3. Study the key signature and name the notes in the following example.

E

MEMORIZE: Flats or sharps in a key signature effect every note on the line or space which they represent unless cancelled by a natural sign.

STUDENT ASSIGNMENT

Date _____

Grade _____

Circle and write the names of the notes effected by the key signature in Exercises 1, 2, and 3.
Count aloud as you tap your foot for each beat – then sing with syllables.

Complete writing the beats under each note and rest in Exercises 4 & 5.   Count – Tap – Sing.

1 an 2 R 4   1   2   3 – 4
   (R=Rest)

1 – 2 an   R   2

Write the letter names under each note in Exercises 6, 7, and 8.

D

Bb

B

Lesson 33

THE FLAT KEYS

Every key signature has a name. When there are no sharps or flats in the key signature we call it the natural key, or key of C. To find the name of any key signature containing flats, count down four letters beginning with the last flat. The last flat is the one farthest to the right. When two or more flats are in the key signature, the flat before the last flat is the name of the key. This is a short cut that will prove very helpful.

THE FLAT KEYS

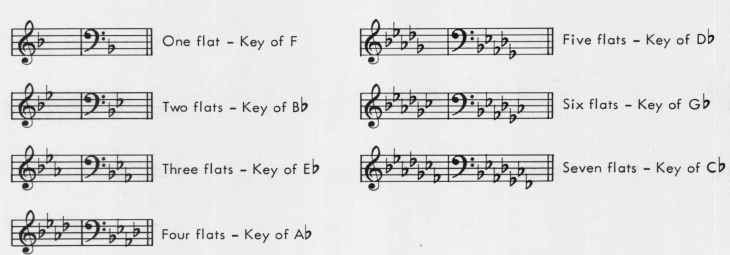

One flat – Key of F

Two flats – Key of B♭

Three flats – Key of E♭

Four flats – Key of A♭

Five flats – Key of D♭

Six flats – Key of G♭

Seven flats – Key of C♭

STUDENT ASSIGNMENT

Date _____

Grade _____

1. No sharps or flats in the key signature is the key of _____ .

2. Four letters below A♭ will be the key of _____ .

3. In the key of A♭ the following notes are always played flat _____ .

4. When all B – E – A – D – G and C's are flat, the key is _____ .

MEMORIZE: The seven flat key signatures, and the notes that are flat in each key.

Lesson 34 (Review)

37

STUDENT ASSIGNMENT

Date _____

Grade _____

Name the key and write the letter name under each note in Exercises 1, 2, and 3.
Count aloud as you tap your foot for each beat — then sing with syllables.

1 Key of _____

2 Key of _____

3 Key of _____

Complete writing the beats under each note and rest in Exercises 4 and 5. Count – Tap – Sing.

4   1—2 R   1 an 2

5   R an 2 an R an R an

Name the key and circle the notes effected by the key signature in Exercises 6, 7, and 8.

6 Key of _____

7 Key of _____

8 Key of _____

L-174

THE SHARP KEYS

To find the name of any key signature containing sharps, count up to the next line or space above the last sharp. The last sharp is the one farthest to the right. Whenever the line or space above the last sharp contains a sharp in the signature, then the word "sharp" is used with the letter name.

THE SHARP KEYS

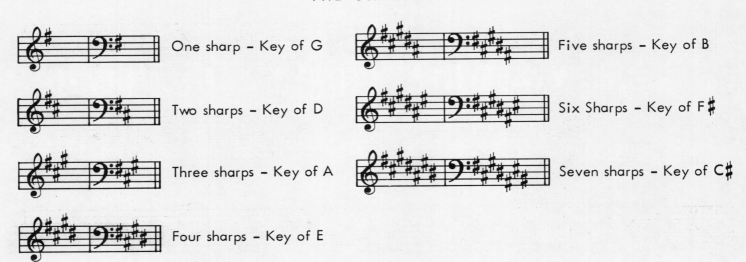

One sharp – Key of G

Two sharps – Key of D

Three sharps – Key of A

Four sharps – Key of E

Five sharps – Key of B

Six Sharps – Key of F♯

Seven sharps – Key of C♯

STUDENT ASSIGNMENT

Date _____

Grade _____

1. If the last sharp is G, the key signature is _____ .

2. In the key of D the following notes are always played sharp _____ .

3. When all F – C – G – D and A's are sharp, the key signature is _____ .

4. Name all notes that are sharp in the key of F♯ _____ .

MEMORIZE: The seven sharp key signatures, and the notes that are sharp in each key.

STUDENT ASSIGNMENT

Date _____

Grade _____

Name the key and write the letter name under each note in Exercises 1, 2, and 3.
Count aloud as you tap your foot for each beat – then sing with syllables.

1 Key of _____

2 Key of _____

3 Key of _____

Draw in the missing bar lines in Ex.4 and 5. Then write the beats. Count – Tap – Sing.

4

5

Name the key and circle the notes effected by the key signature in Exercises 6, 7, and 8.

6 Key of _____

7 Key of _____

8 Key of _____

L-174

SIXTEENTH NOTES

Add two flags to the stem of a quarter note (♩) and it becomes a sixteenth note (♬). Two

sixteenth notes equal one eighth note: ♬ ♬ = ♪ ;therefore, four sixteenth notes equal one

quarter note: ♬♬♬♬ = ♩ Whenever a quarter note is equal to one beat (as in $\frac{2}{4}$-$\frac{3}{4}$-$\frac{4}{4}$ time),

a sixteenth note is equal to one-fourth of a beat.

$$♩ \quad = \quad ♬ \quad + \quad ♬ \quad + \quad ♬ \quad + \quad ♬$$

$$\text{beat} \rightarrow 1 \quad = \quad \tfrac{1}{4} \quad + \quad \tfrac{1}{4} \quad + \quad \tfrac{1}{4} \quad + \quad \tfrac{1}{4}$$

When two or more sixteenth notes are next to one another like this: ♬♬♬♬ they may be

written like this: ♬ ♬ or like this: ♬♬♬♬

The beats under the sixteenth notes may be written like this:—

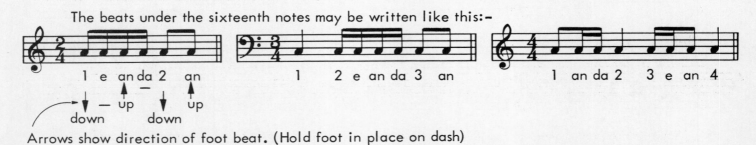

1 e an da 2 an   1   2 e an da 3 an   1 an da 2   3 e an 4

down — up down up

Arrows show direction of foot beat. (Hold foot in place on dash)

STUDENT ASSIGNMENT

Date _____

Grade _____

1. On the staff below write four sixteenth notes and one quarter note in the first measure.
2. Write two eighth notes and four sixteenth notes in the second measure.
3. Write four sixteenth notes and two eighth notes in the third measure.
4. Write eight sixteenth notes in the fourth measure.

5. Write the beats under each note that you have placed on the staff.

> MEMORIZE: Tap your foot "down" on the beat numbers and "up" on the an.
> (Never down on e – an – da.)

STUDENT ASSIGNMENT

Date _____

Grade _____

Write the beats under each note and rest in Ex.1 through 4.
Then count the time aloud while tapping your foot.

1

2

3

4

Write the notes and rests represented by the beats below the line in Ex.5 through 8.
Then count the time aloud while tapping your foot.

5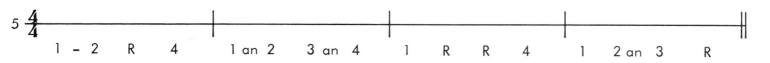

6

7

8

SIXTEENTH RESTS

The sixteenth rest also has two flags. These are sixteenth rests: ꜞ ꜞ ꜞ ꜞ Two sixteenth rests equal one eighth rest: ꜞ ꜞ = ꜞ Therefore, four sixteenth rests equal one quarter rest: ꜞ ꜞ ꜞ ꜞ = 𝄽 Whenever a quarter rest is equal to one beat (as in $\frac{2}{4}$ - $\frac{3}{4}$ - $\frac{4}{4}$ time) a sixteenth rest is equal to one-fourth of a beat.

$$𝄽 = ꜞ + ꜞ + ꜞ + ꜞ$$

$$\text{beat} \rightarrow 1 = \tfrac{1}{4} + \tfrac{1}{4} + \tfrac{1}{4} + \tfrac{1}{4}$$

The beats under these sixteenth notes and sixteenth rests may be written like this:-

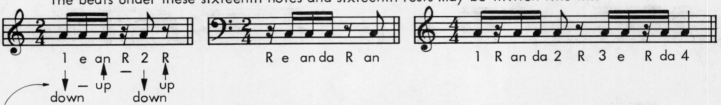

1 e an R 2 R   R e an da R an   1 R an da 2 R 3 e R da 4

down — up — down up

Arrows show direction of foot beat. (Hold foot in place on dash.)

STUDENT ASSIGNMENT

Date _____

Grade _____

1. On the staff below fill in the first measure with as many ꜞ ♬ as needed.

2. Fill in the second measure with as many ♩ ꜞ ♩ as needed.

3. Fill in the third measure with as many ♬ ꜞ ♩ as needed.

4. Fill in the fourth measure with as many ♬ ꜞ as needed.

5. Write the beats under each note and rest that you have placed on the staff.

> MEMORIZE: Whenever a quarter note or a quarter rest equals one beat, a sixteenth note or a sixteenth rest equals one-fourth beat.

STUDENT ASSIGNMENT

Date _____

Grade _____

Write the beats under each note in Ex.1 through 4.
Then count the time aloud while tapping your foot.

Write the notes and rests represented by the beats below the line in Ex.5 through 8.
Then count the time aloud while tapping your foot.

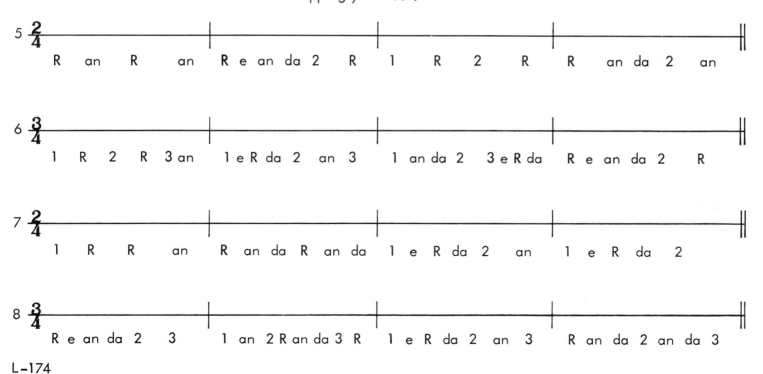

Lesson 41
DOTTED EIGHTH NOTES

In Lessons 13 and 25 in Book One we learned that a dot placed after any note is equal to one-half the value of the note it follows. Therefore: whenever an eighth note receives one-half beat (as in $\frac{2}{4}$ - $\frac{3}{4}$ - $\frac{4}{4}$ time) a dotted eighth note receives three-quarters of a beat. An eighth note (♪) receives 1/2 beat. The dot (•) half of this or 1/4 beat. The two together receive 3/4 of a beat. Or: since an eighth note is equal to two sixteenth notes (♪ = ♬) a dotted eighth note is equal to three sixteenth notes (♪• = ♪ ♪ ♪).

The beats under the dotted eighth notes may be written like this:

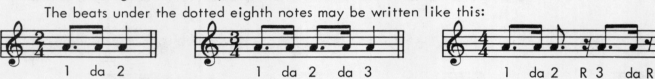

STUDENT ASSIGNMENT

Date _____

Grade _____

1. How many sixteenth notes equal one dotted eighth note ? _____

2. If the time signature is $\frac{4}{4}$, how much of a beat does a dotted eighth note receive ? _____

3. Write the beats under each note and rest in the following exercises.

MEMORIZE: A dotted eighth note equals three sixteenth notes. Whenever an eighth note receives one-half beat a dotted eighth note receives three-fourths of a beat.

ALLA BREVE

The letter **C** is often used for the time signature. It is called common time and
and means exactly the same as $\frac{4}{4}$ time.

When a vertical line is drawn through the common time letter (¢) the value of both the
upper number four (4) and the lower number four (4) is cut in half and the time signature becomes $\frac{2}{2}$.

This is known in music as ALLA BREVE, also called CUT TIME.

Therefore ¢ or $\frac{2}{2}$ means there are two beats in each measure (top number 2) and
that a half note receives one beat (bottom number 2).

In Alla Breve, or Cut Time, the beats may be written under the notes like this:

1 – 2   1   2   1   an   2   an   1   e   an   da   2   e   an   da

STUDENT ASSIGNMENT

Date _____

Grade _____

1. How many beats are there in each measure of ¢ ? _____

2. How many beats does a half note receive in Alla Breve ? _____

3. What note receives one half beat in Cut Time ? _____

4. What note receives one fourth beat in Alla Breve? _____

5. Write the beats under each note in the following exercise.

6. From what famous march are these 8 measures taken? _____

MEMORIZE: The time signature ¢ is called ALLA BREVE or CUT TIME and means exactly
the same as $\frac{2}{2}$ time. (2 beats to each measure and a half note receives 1 beat)

Lesson 43 (Review)

STUDENT ASSIGNMENT

Date _____

Grade _____

Write the beats under each note and rest in Ex.1 through 3.
Then count time aloud while tapping your foot.

Write the notes and rests represented by the count below the line in Ex.4 through 6.
Then count time aloud while tapping your foot.

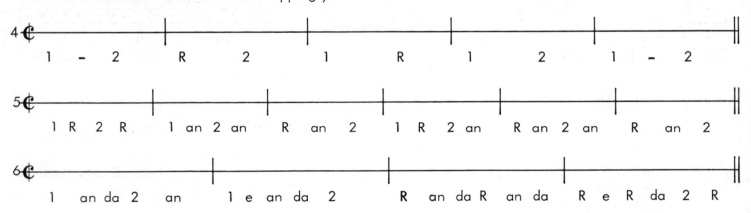

Name the key – circle the notes affected by the key signature – write the beats under each note in Ex.7 through 9.

7 Key of _____

8 Key of _____

9 Key of _____

L-174

INTERVALS

An interval in music is the distance between two tones with regard to pitch.   The interval is counted from the lower note to the upper, including both. Intervals remain the same whether we use the treble clef staff, or the bass clef staff.

In the following exercise we have intervals which have been written above the key tone C. Always count the bottom tone as number one (1).

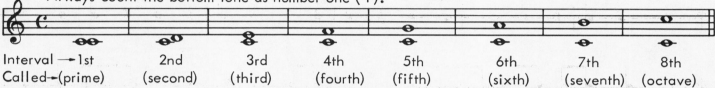

| Interval → 1st | 2nd | 3rd | 4th | 5th | 6th | 7th | 8th |
| Called → (prime) | (second) | (third) | (fourth) | (fifth) | (sixth) | (seventh) | (octave) |

In the next exercise we have intervals which have been written above the key tone C in bass clef.

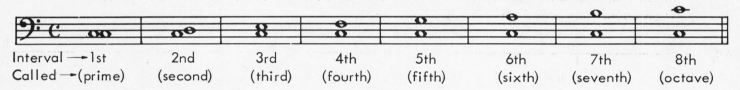

| Interval → 1st | 2nd | 3rd | 4th | 5th | 6th | 7th | 8th |
| Called → (prime) | (second) | (third) | (fourth) | (fifth) | (sixth) | (seventh) | (octave) |

STUDENT ASSIGNMENT

Date _____

Grade _____

1. In the key of G the interval from G up to D is ? _____

2. In the key of A♭ the interval from A♭ up to C is ? _____

3. In the key of D the interval from D up to E is ? _____

4. Write the interval name under the notes in the following exercise.

MEMORIZE: The interval is the distance between two tones with regard to pitch. Always count the bottom tone as number one (1) and count up to include the note above.

Lesson 45

WHOLE and HALF STEPS

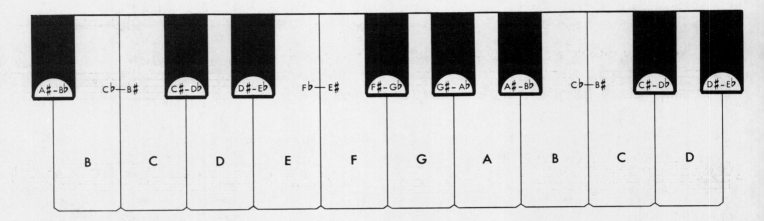

In the partial keyboard above you will notice black keys in between all white keys, except between B – C and E – F. These black keys represent half steps either above or below the white keys. The distance between B – C and E – F is also a half step. Therefore:

From any key to the key above or below is one-half step.
    Example: (B to C) (C to C♯) (A to A♭).
From any key two half steps above or below is a whole step.
    Example: (C to C♯ to D) (F♯ to F to E) (C to B to B♭).
From any key three half steps above or below is a step and one-half.
    Example: (F to E to E♭ to D) (G to G♯ to A to A♯) (B to C to C♯ to D).

STUDENT ASSIGNMENT

Date _____

Grade _____

1. How many steps are there between F and the F♯ above? _____

2. How many steps are there between A and the G below? _____

3. How many steps are there between C and the A below? _____

4. What is the name of the note one whole step above B ? _____

5. What is the name of the note a step and one-half below D ? _____

MEMORIZE: The distance between (E – F) and (B – C) is one-half step. Between all other natural notes the distance is one whole step.

STUDENT ASSIGNMENT

Date _____

Grade _____

Write the interval under the notes in Exercises 1 through 4.

Write the second note to complete the intervals in Exercises 5 through 8.

Build half steps – whole steps – step and one-half – up ↑ or down ↓ from the following notes in Exercises 9 through 12.

Mark the following as half step – whole step or step and one-half.

Lesson 47

TETRACHORDS

The early Greeks devised scales which had only four notes, or tones. These scales were called TETRACHORDS, the word "Tetra" meaning four. The tetrachord progression of ascending tones is as follows: whole step – whole step – half step, or 1 – 1 – 1/2.

An ascending tetrachord starting on the tone C would appear like this:-

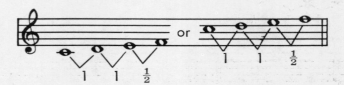

An ascending tetrachord starting on the tone E would appear like this:-

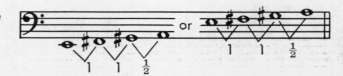

An ascending tetrachord starting on the tone B♭ would appear like this:-

STUDENT ASSIGNMENT

| Date |
| Grade |

1. A tetrachord consists of _____ tones.

2. Name the notes of an ascending tetrachord starting on F. _____

3. Name the notes of an ascending tetrachord starting on G. _____

4. Name the notes of an ascending tetrachord starting on A♭ . _____

5. Name the notes of an ascending tetrachord starting on D♭ . _____

MEMORIZE: An ascending tetrachord is a progression of four notes which follow the pattern: whole step – whole step – half step or 1 – 1 – 1/2.

STUDENT ASSIGNMENT

Date _____

Grade _____

Study Exercise 1 carefully.
Build ascending tetrachords marking the whole and half steps in Exercises 2 through 4.

Write the intervals under the notes in Ex.5.

Write the note to complete these intervals

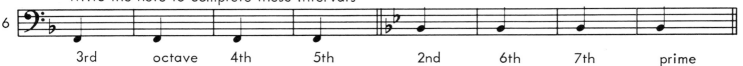

Build half steps – whole steps – step and one-half – up ↑ or down ↓ from the following notes in Exercise 7.

Mark the following as half step – whole step or step and one-half.

L-174

Lesson 49

MAJOR SCALES

A scale is a succession of tones ascending or descending from a given note to its octave according to a specified pattern.

A major scale consists of two tetrachords with the interval of a whole tone or step between. Therefore, a major scale is a progression of eight notes to the octave, which follows the following pattern:

ASCENDING

1 step-1 step-½ step - 1 step - 1 step-1 step-½ step

or

1 - 1 - ½ - 1 - 1 - 1 - ½

DESCENDING

½ step-1 step-1 step - 1 step - ½ step-1 step-1 step

or

½ - 1 - 1 - 1 - ½ - 1 - 1

This is a major scale starting on C.

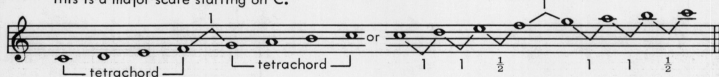

This a major scale starting on D.

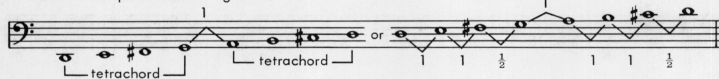

STUDENT ASSIGNMENT

Date _____

Grade _____

1. How many notes are there in a major scale including the octave? _____

2. How many tetrachords are needed to make one major scale? _____

3. Is the interval between tetrachords of a major scale a whole step or half step? _____

4. Write a major scale in two octaves starting on E♭ and mark the whole and half steps.

MEMORIZE: A major scale consists of two tetrachords with the interval of a whole tone, or step between.

STUDENT ASSIGNMENT

Date _____

Grade _____

In Exercises 2, 3, and 4 build major scales ascending and descending, using the proper accidentals. Study example number one first.

Write the major scales ascending and descending for the key signatures shown in Ex.5 and 6.

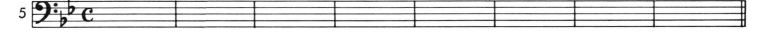

Build major scales ascending and descending on the following notes and place the correct flats and sharps in the key signature.

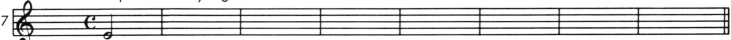

Lesson 51

CIRCLE OF KEYS

The second, or upper tetrachord of any ascending major scale becomes the first, or lower tetrachord of a new major scale whose name is derived from the first note, or tone of that tetrachord.

Example:

Therefore, the fifth note, or tone of any ascending major scale (which is the first note of the second tetrachord) is the beginning of a new major scale.

The scale starting a fifth above C is the G major scale with one sharp.
The scale starting a fifth above G is the D major scale with two sharps.
The scale starting a fifth above D is the A major scale with three sharps.
The scale starting a fifth above A is the E major scale with four sharps.
The scale starting a fifth above E is the B major scale with five sharps.
The scale starting a fifth above B is the F♯ major scale with six sharps.
The scale starting a fifth above F♯ is the C♯ major scale with seven sharps.

STUDENT ASSIGNMENT

Date	
Grade	

1. A fifth above G is the _____ major scale with _____ sharps.

2. A fifth above D is the _____ major scale with _____ sharps.

3. A fifth above A is the _____ major scale with _____ sharps.

4. A fifth above E is the _____ major scale with _____ sharps.

5. A fifth above B is the _____ major scale with _____ sharps.

6. A fifth above F♯ is the _____ major scale with _____ sharps.

MEMORIZE: Starting with the scale of C major the fifth note, or tone of each scale is used as the beginning of a new major scale.

CIRCLE OF KEYS
(CONTINUED)

The second, or lower tetrachord of any descending major scale becomes the first, or upper tetrachord of a new major scale whose name is derived from the first note, or tone of that tetrachord.

Example:

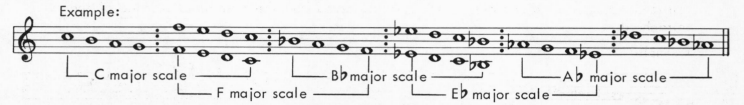

Therefore, the fifth note, or tone of any descending major scale (which is the first note of the second tetrachord) is the beginning of a new major scale.

The scale starting a fifth below C is the F major scale with one flat.
The scale starting a fifth below F is the B♭ major scale with two flats.
The scale starting a fifth below B♭ is the E♭ major scale with three flats.
The scale starting a fifth below E♭ is the A♭ major scale with four flats.
The scale starting a fifth below A♭ is the D♭ major scale with five flats.
The scale starting a fifth below D♭ is the G♭ major scale with six flats.
The scale starting a fifth below G♭ is the C♭ major scale with seven flats.

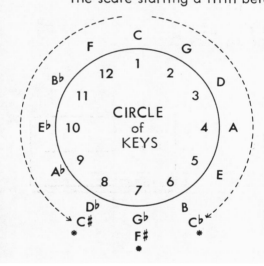

Beginning on C and going clockwise, we have the sharp keys (ascending tetrachords). Counter clockwise from C, we have the flat keys (descending tetrachords). We can now see that all major keys have a relationship by the way of the Circle of Keys.

✳ The major scales of (B and C♭) have the same tonal sound and are played on the same keys of the piano. This is also true of the major scales of (G♭ and F♯) and (D♭ and C♯).

STUDENT ASSIGNMENT

| Date _____ |
| Grade _____ |

1. A fifth below F is the _____ major scale with _____ flats.

2. A fifth below A♭ is the _____ major scale with _____ flats.

3. A fifth below C is the _____ major scale with _____ flat.

MEMORIZE: The complete Circle of Keys, also known as the Circle of Fifths.

C - G - D - A - E - B - G♭ - D♭ - A♭ - E♭ - B♭ - F - C

Lesson 53 (Review)

STUDENT ASSIGNMENT

Date _____

Grade _____

Write the interval under each of the following:

Build half steps – whole steps – step and a half – up↑ or down↓ from the following notes in Ex.3.

Mark the following as half step – whole step or step and one-half.

Build ascending tetrachords using the starting notes in Ex. 5 and 6. Then write the letter names under each note.

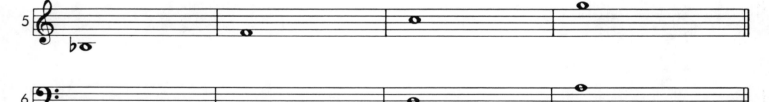

Build major scales ascending and descending on the following notes and place the correct flats and sharps in the key signature.

L-174

STUDENT ASSIGNMENT

Put in the clef sign, write the proper key signature as indicated below and place the starting note of the scale in Exercises 1 through 4.

Write the name of the key below these examples and place the starting note of the scale in Exercises 5 through 8.

Lesson 55

$$\frac{3}{8} - \frac{6}{8} - \frac{9}{8} - \frac{12}{8}$$

(In Slow Time)

In Lesson 9 (Book 1) we learned that the lower number in the time signature determines the value of each note or rest. Study the following examples:

In $\frac{2}{2}$ time the half note (𝅗𝅥) or half rest (▬) receives one beat.

In $\frac{3}{4}$ time the quarter note (♩) or quarter rest (𝄽) receives one beat.

In $\frac{6}{8}$ time the eighth note (♪) or eighth rest (𝄾) receives one beat.

Slow time note and rest values when the time signature is $\frac{3}{8} - \frac{6}{8} - \frac{9}{8} - \frac{12}{8}$

♪ or 𝄾 = ½ beat   ♪ or 𝄾 = 1 beat   ♩ or 𝄽 = 2 beats

♩. or 𝄽. = 3 beats   𝅗𝅥 or ▬ = 4 beats   𝅗𝅥. or ▬• = 6 beats

The beats may be written under the notes and rests in slow time like this:

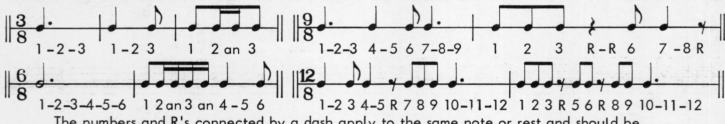

The numbers and R's connected by a dash apply to the same note or rest and should be counted in a continuous sound.

STUDENT ASSIGNMENT

1. Write the beats under each note and rest in slow time.

MEMORIZE: When the lower number of the time signature is 8, the note values in slow time are: ♪ = ½ beat; ♪ = 1 beat; ♩. = 3 beats; 𝅗𝅥. = 6 beats.

STUDENT ASSIGNMENT

Date _____

Grade _____

Write the beats under each note and rest in Ex.1 through 4 in slow time. Count – Tap – Sing.

Draw the missing bar lines, then write the beats under each note and rest in Ex.5 through 8 in slow time.

Lesson 57

$$\frac{3}{8} - \frac{6}{8} - \frac{9}{8} - \frac{12}{8}$$

(In Fast Time)

In Lesson 42 we learned that we could change $\frac{4}{4}$ time to C or $\frac{2}{2}$ time. From slow time to fast time. We can perform a similar change from slow time to fast time for $\frac{3}{8} - \frac{6}{8} - \frac{9}{8} - \frac{12}{8}$ time by dividing both the top number of beats per measure (3-6-9-12) and the value of the eighth note (lower number 8) by 3, giving the eighth note (♪)1/3 beat.

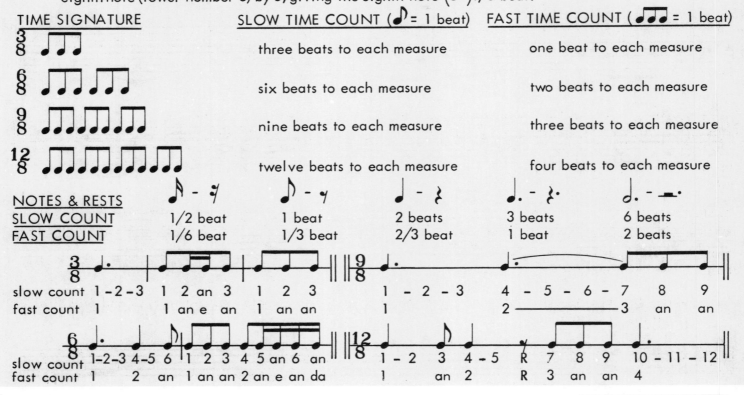

STUDENT ASSIGNMENT

Date _____

Grade _____

1. Write the beats under each note and rest in the following exercise in fast time.

2. Draw the missing bar lines in the following exercise and write the beats in fast time.

MEMORIZE: When the lower number of the time signature is **8**, the note values in fast time are: ♪ = 1/3 beat; ♩ = 2/3 beat; ♩. = 1 beat; ♩. = 2 beats.

STUDENT ASSIGNMENT

Date _____

Grade _____

Write the beats under each note and rest in Ex.1 through 4. First in slow time and then in fast time.

Draw the missing bar lines, then write the beats under each note and rest in Ex.5 and 6 in slow time then in fast time.

Lesson 59

SYNCOPATION

Special effects may be acquired in music by placing special accents (>) or emphasis on different beats or parts of a beat. Whenever a natural accent or strong beat is moved from its natural place to a weak beat, usually by means of tying over a note from a weak beat to a strong beat, we have syncopation.

Here are some examples of syncopation showing you how to write the beats below and the accent marks (>) above the notes.

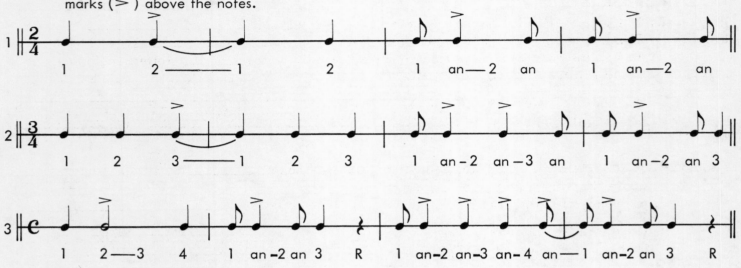

STUDENT ASSIGNMENT

Date _____

Grade _____

Write the beats under the notes and the accents above the syncopated notes in these exercises.

Count – Tap – Sing.

MEMORIZE: To accent (>) is to place force on a tone or beat. Syncopation means accenting tones, or beats which are normally unaccented.

STUDENT TEST

Date _____

Grade _____

Lesson 31 1. Sharps and flats immediately following the Clef sign are called _____ _____ .

2. The effect of the Key Signature lasts to the _____ of the piece of music, or until a change to another _____ .

3. To cancel a sharp or flat on any note we use a _____ sign.

Lesson 33 1. The natural key, no sharps or flats, is called the key of _____ .

2. To find the name of any key containing flats we count down _____ letters beginning with the last flat.

3. Write the key signatures in the following examples:

Eb   Ab   F   Db

Lesson 35 1. To find the name of any key containing sharps we count _____ to the next line or space above the last _____ .

2. In the key of A the following notes are raised one half-step _____ .

3. Write the key signatures in the following examples:

D   E   A   C

Lesson 37 1. A quarter note equals _____ sixteenth notes.

2. When counting time for a group of four sixteenth notes in $\frac{2}{4}$ - $\frac{3}{4}$ or $\frac{4}{4}$ time, we say _____ for the second 16th and _____ for the fourth 16th.

3. Write the beats under the following example:

Lesson 39 1. It takes _____ sixteenth rests to equal one eighth rest.

2. In $\frac{2}{4}$ - $\frac{3}{4}$ or $\frac{4}{4}$ time, a sixteenth rest or note equals _____ beat.

3. Write the beats under the following example:

Lesson 41 1. A dotted eighth note equals _____ sixteenth notes.

2. In $\frac{2}{4}$ - $\frac{3}{4}$ or $\frac{4}{4}$ time, a dotted eighth note receives _____ of a beat.

3. A _____ note or rest usually follows a dotted eighth note.

Lesson 42 1. In the time signature the letter C stands for _____ time.

2. A line through the letter ¢ stands for _____ or _____ time.

3. In alla breve, or cut time, a half note receives _____ beat.

Lesson 44 1. The distance between two tones with regard to pitch is called an _____ .

2. To find the interval between two tones we start with the _____ tone and count _____ .

3. Write the interval name under the following:

Lesson 60 (continued)

STUDENT TEST

Date _____

Grade _____

Lesson 45 1. The distance between C and D above or F and G above is a _____ step.
2. The distance between E and G above is a _____ .
3. The distance between F and E below or C and B below is a _____ step.

Lesson 47 1. There are _____ tones in a tetrachord.
2. The ascending pattern of the tetrachord is _____ step, _____ step, _____ step.

3. Write a tetrachord on the following notes:

Lesson 49 1. Including the octave, there are _____ tones in a major scale.
2. The ascending pattern of a major scale is: _____ step, _____ step, _____ step, _____ step, _____ step, _____ step, _____ step.
3. A major scale consists of _____ tetrachords with the interval of a _____ step between them.

Lesson 51 1. Starting a fifth above G is the _____ Major scale with _____ sharps.
2. Starting a fifth above F is the _____ Major scale with _____ flats or sharps.
3. Starting a fifth above A♭ is the _____ Major scale with _____ flats.

Lesson 52 1. Starting a fifth below B♭ is the _____ Major scale with _____ flats.
2. Starting a fifth below G is the _____ Major scale with _____ flats or sharps.
3. Starting a fifth below E is the _____ Major scale with _____ sharps.

Lesson 55 1. In slow $\frac{6}{8}$ - $\frac{9}{8}$ or $\frac{12}{8}$ time, an eighth note receives _____ beat; a dotted quarter note receives _____ beats; a dotted half note receives _____ beats.

2. There are _____ dotted quarter notes in one measure of slow $\frac{9}{8}$ time.

3. Write the beats under the following slow time example:

Lesson 57 1. In fast $\frac{6}{8}$ - $\frac{9}{8}$ or $\frac{12}{8}$ time, an eighth note receives _____ beat; a dotted quarter note receives _____ beat; a dotted half note receives _____ beats.

2. There are 12 eighth notes in a measure of _____ time.

3. Write the beats under the following fast time example:

Lesson 59 1. This mark ＞ placed over or under a note, is called an _____ .
2. To accent means to place _____ on a tone or beat.
3. Whenever natural accents or strong beats do NOT fall in their proper places, we have _____ .